# God's Promises in 8 Key Life Areas

## That Will Change Your Life!

*By Krystal Kuehn and Violet James*

**MP**
Maximum Potential, LLC

Cover Design by Violet James

© 2014 Maximum Potential, LLC
All Rights Reserved.
Printed in USA


No part of this book may be reproduced or transmitted in any form or by any means, electronic or mechanical, including photocopying, recording, or by any information storage and retrieval system, without permission in writing from the publisher.


Unless otherwise indicated, all Scripture quotations are taken from the New King James Version. Copyright © 1982 by Thomas Nelson, Inc. All rights reserved. Used by permission.


Legal Notice: This book is intended for personal growth and development. It is not intended to take the place of professional counseling or consulting. While all attempts have been made to verify information provided in this publication, neither the Author nor the Publisher assumes any responsibility for errors, omissions, or contrary interpretation of the subject matter herein. The Purchaser of this publication assumes responsibility for the use of these materials and information. Adherence to all applicable laws and regulations, federal, state, and local, governing professional licensing, business practices, advertising, and all other aspects of doing business in the United States or any other jurisdiction is the sole responsibility of the Purchaser or Reader. The Author and Publisher assume no responsibility or liability whatsoever on the behalf of any Purchaser or Reader of these materials.

You can download *God's Promises in 8 Key Life Areas...* in AUDIO version and listen on your Kindle™ tablet, iPhone®, iPod®, and Android™. Download it at Amazon.com or Audible.com or iTunes.

*"We have everything we need to live a life that pleases God. It was all given to us by God's own power, when we learned that He invited us to share in His wonderful goodness. God made great and marvelous promises, so that His nature would become part of us. Then we could escape our evil desires and the corrupt influences of this world."*

*2 Peter 1:3-4, CEV*

# Table of Contents

**Introduction**

**Chapter One:**

*The Foundation: My Relationship with God*     1

**Chapter Two:**

*Jesus Came to Give Me Abundant Life*     5

**Chapter Three:**

*KEY LIFE AREA #1:*

*God gives me...Love for Life, Self and Others*     9

**Chapter Four**

*KEY LIFE AREA #2:*

*God gives me... Purpose in Living*     13

**Chapter Five**

*KEY LIFE AREA #3:*

*God gives me... Enduring Hope*     17

**Chapter Six**

*KEY LIFE AREA #4:*

*God gives me...Perfect Peace*     21

**Chapter Seven**

*KEY LIFE AREA #5:*

*God helps me to have a... Positive Thought Life*     25

**Chapter Eight**

*KEY LIFE AREA #6:*

*God helps me to have a... Healthy Self-Image*     *29*

**Chapter Nine**

*KEY LIFE AREA #7:*

*God provides... Inner Healing of My Soul*     *33*

**Chapter Ten**

*KEY LIFE AREA #8:*

*God gives me... A Thankful Heart*     *37*

**Conclusion**     41

**About the Authors**     43

# Introduction

There is no area in our lives in which we cannot apply God's truth. God's promises provide all we need or seek after: comfort, guidance, hope, peace, love, strength, healing, encouragement, joy, etc. However, in order to experience the reality of God in our lives, we must have a personal relationship with Him.

Our relationship with God is the very foundation upon which we can change and become all He wants us to be. It is God's plan that we live in the abundance of His grace and goodness. Our responsibility is to know Him, receive His promises, and walk in His truth. As we do, we will be changed from the inside out. God's word will change our lives forever!

Following are Scriptures of God's promises of who we are in Christ applied to (8) key life areas. It begins with the foundation—our relationship with God, followed by God's desire that we live our life in Him to the fullest. As we explore each key life area, you will be able to identify areas that may be keeping you from God's best for your life. By internalizing who you are in Christ, you will be changed by the power of God's word.

May the truth of who you are in Christ help you to grow closer to God and enjoy your journey with Him.

Krystal and Violet

# Chapter One:

## *The Foundation:*
## *My Relationship with God*

The basis for living the abundant life that God intended for us to live starts with a personal, intimate relationship with God. God not only wants us to know Him as our Creator and Savior, He also wants us to know Him as our Heavenly Father, closest friend, and first love.

*In Christ...*

## I am saved

*I confess with my mouth, "Jesus is Lord," and believe in my heart that God raised him from the dead, and I am saved (Rom. 10:9, NIV). God saved me by his special favor when I believed. And I can't take credit for this; it is a gift from God. Salvation is not a reward for the good things I have done, so I can't boast about it (Eph. 2:8, 9, NLT).*

## I am forgiven

*When I was dead in my sins and the uncircumcision of my sinful nature, God made me alive with Christ. He forgave all my sins, having cancelled the written code, with its regulations, that was against me and that stood opposed to me; he took it away nailing it to the cross (Col. 2:13, 14, NIV).*

# I am a child of God

*Because I am a child of God (son/daughter), God sent the Spirit of his Son into my heart, the Spirit who calls out, "Abba, Father." So I am no longer a slave, but a child of God; and since I am a child of God, God has made me also an heir (Gal. 4:6, 7, NIV).*

## *Reflections & Prayers*

## Chapter Two:

### *Jesus Came to Give Me Abundant Life*

Jesus died for us so that we can enjoy life and receive all the promises and blessings that are made available to us as His children. He wants us to live our life to the fullest with true fulfillment in Him.

*In Christ…*

## I am fulfilled

*The thief comes only in order to steal and kill and destroy. Jesus came that I may have and enjoy life, and have it in abundance (to the full, till it overflows) (John 10:10, Amp.)*

## I am prosperous

*My delight and desire are in the law of the Lord, and on His law—the precepts, the instructions, the teachings of God—I habitually meditate (ponder and study) by day and by night. I shall be like a tree firmly planted (and tended) by the streams of water, ready to bring forth its fruit in its season; its leaf also shall not fade or wither, and everything I do shall prosper (and come to maturity) (Ps. 1:2, 3, Amp.)*

## I am joyful

*I have not seen Christ, but still I love him. I cannot see him now, but I believe in him. So I am filled with a joy that cannot be explained, a joy full of glory (1 Peter 1:8, NCV).*

### *Reflections & Prayers*

# Chapter Three:

## KEY LIFE AREA #1:

### God gives me...
### Love for Life, Self and Others

---

God is love and nothing can separate us from His love. When we have a relationship with Him, we are able to receive His love and love Him in return with all our heart. Barriers in our hearts such as unforgiveness, bitterness, offenses, anger, etc., block our ability to receive God's love. When the barriers are removed, His love freely flows through us to love life, self and others.

*In Christ…*

## I am rooted and grounded in love

*Lord, strengthen me with might through Your Spirit in the inner man…that being rooted and grounded in love…I may know the love of Christ which passes knowledge and that I may be filled with all the fullness of God (Eph. 3:16-19).*

## I am loved

*For I am persuaded that neither death nor life, nor things present nor things to come, nor height nor depth, nor any other created thing, shall be able to separate me from the love of God which is in Christ Jesus my Lord (Romans 8:38, 39).*

## I am loving

*I love others, for love is of God and I am born of God and know God (1 John 4:7, 8).*

*Reflections & Prayers*

# Chapter Four:

## *KEY LIFE AREA #2:*

### *God gives me...*
### *Purpose in Living*

God leads and guides us concerning His will, plan, and purpose for our life. He directs our every step as we trust in Him. He shows us the path of life.

*In Christ…*

## I am significant

*Christ gives meaning to my life (Christ is my life) (Col. 3:4a, CEV). I have been crucified with Christ; it is no longer I who live, but Christ lives in me; and the life which I now live in the flesh I live by faith in the Son of God who loved me and gave Himself for me (Gal. 2:20).*

## I am purposeful

*"For I know the plans I have for you," declares the Lord, "plans to prosper you and not to harm you, plans to give you hope and a future" (Jeremiah 29:11, NIV).*

## I am God's workmanship

*For I am God's (own) handiwork (His workmanship), recreated in Christ Jesus, (born anew) that I may do those good works which God predestined (planned beforehand) for me, (taking paths which He prepared ahead of time) that I should walk in them— living the good life which He prearranged and made ready for me to live (Eph. 2:10, Amp.).*

## *Reflections & Prayers*

# Chapter Five:

## *KEY LIFE AREA #3:*

### *God gives me...*
### *Enduring Hope*

We have an ever-living hope. Because Jesus was raised from the dead, we have been given a brand new life. And we have everything we need to live for Him here on earth as well as a glorious future in heaven to look forward to.

*In Christ…*

## I am hopeful

*The God of hope fills me with all joy and peace in believing, that I may abound in hope by the power of the Holy Spirit (Romans 15:13). And now Lord, what do I wait for and expect? My hope and expectation are in You (Ps. 39:7, Amp.).*

## I am faithfilled

*I live by faith, not by sight (2 Cor. 5:7). By faith, I believe that God exists and that He cares enough to respond to me as I seek Him (Hebrews 11:6, Msg.).*

## I am trusting God

*I wait for the Lord, my soul waits, and in His word I do hope (Ps. 130:5). But as for me, I trust in You, O Lord; I say, "You are my*

*God." My times are in Your hand (Ps. 31:14, 15a).*

## *Reflections & Prayers*

# Chapter Six:

## *KEY LIFE AREA #4:*

### *God gives me...*
### *Perfect Peace*

---

Jesus is the source of true peace. He is the Prince of Peace. We can have God's perfect peace not only when everything is going well in our life but also when you are in the midst of trails and storms. As we keep our minds focused on Him, He will keep us in perfect peace.

*In Christ…*

## I am carefree

*I don't worry about anything, but I pray about everything. With a thankful heart I offer up my prayers and requests to God; and the peace of God, which surpasses all understanding, will guard my heart and mind through Christ Jesus (Phil. 4:6, 7, CEV, NKJV).*

## I am sound minded

*I let the peace of God rule in my heart (Col. 3:15b, NCV). God has not given me a spirit of fear, but of power and of love and of a sound mind (2 Timothy 1:7).*

## I am a peacemaker

*I want to enjoy life and see good days ahead…so I search for peace—harmony; undisturbedness from fears, agitating passions and moral conflicts—and seek it eagerly. I do not merely desire peaceful relations [with God, with my fellowmen, and with myself], but I pursue and go after them! (1 Peter 3:10, 11, Amp.).*

## *Reflections & Prayers*

# Chapter Seven:

## *KEY LIFE AREA #5:*

## *God helps me to have a...*
## *Positive Thought Life*

---

Developing a positive thought life starts with renewing our mind. When God lives inside of us, we are spiritually reborn. However, our mind isn't. It must be renewed daily by studying, meditating, and applying God's word.

*In Christ…*

## I am positive and optimistic

*I fill my mind and meditate on things true, noble, reputable, authentic, compelling, gracious—the best, not the worst; the beautiful, not the ugly; things to praise, not things to curse (Phil. 4:8, Msg.).*

## I am renewed

*…with regard to my former way of life, I put off my old self, which is being corrupted by its deceitful desires; I am made new in the attitude of my mind; and I put on the new self, created to be like God in true righteousness and holiness (Eph. 4:22-24, NIV).*

## I am Christ-minded

*I have the mind of Christ (1 Cor. 2:16b). For though I walk in the flesh, I do not war according to the flesh. For the weapons of our warfare are not carnal but mighty in God for pulling down strongholds, casting down arguments and every high thing that exalts itself against the knowledge of God, bringing every thought into captivity to the obedience of Christ (2 Cor. 10:3-5).*

## Reflections & Prayers

_____
_____
_____
_____
_____
_____
_____
_____
_____
_____
_____
_____
_____
_____
_____

# Chapter Eight:

## *KEY LIFE AREA #6:*

### *God helps me to have a... Healthy Self-Image*

---

As we grow in our relationship with God, we will begin to see ourselves as God sees us. We will continually be conformed to the image and likeness of Christ and reflect His glory.

*In Christ...*

## I am worthy

*Not even a sparrow, worth only half a penny can fall to the ground without my Father knowing it. He pays even greater attention to me, down to the last detail—even numbering the hairs on my head. So I will not be afraid; I am more valuable to him than a whole flock of sparrows (Matt. 10:29-31, NLT, Msg.)*

## I am special

*For You formed my inward parts; You covered me in my mother's womb. I will praise You, for I am fearfully and wonderfully made; marvelous are Your works, and that my soul knows very well (Ps. 139:13, 14).*

## I am Christlike

*...I can be a mirror that brightly reflects the glory of God. And as the Spirit of the Lord*

*works within me, I become more and more like him and reflect his glory even more (2 Cor. 3:18, NLT).*

## *Reflections & Prayers*

# Chapter Nine:

## *KEY LIFE AREA #7:*

## *God provides...*
## *Inner Healing of My Soul*

---

God's grace, mercy and love pour out to us when we cry out to Him. He comforts us when we are hurting and holds us in His everlasting arms of love. He heals our pain and restores our broken heart.

*In Christ…*

## I am restored

*The Lord is close to the brokenhearted and saves those who are crushed in spirit (Ps. 34:18, NIV). He makes me to lie down in green pastures; He leads me beside the still waters. He restores my soul (Ps. 23:2, 3a).*

## I am healed

*He heals the brokenhearted and binds up their wounds (Ps. 147:3). But he was pierced for my transgressions, he was crushed for my iniquities; the punishment that brought me peace was upon him, and by his wounds I am healed (Isaiah 53:5, NIV).*

## I am free

*Jesus said…if I abide in His word, I am His disciple indeed. And I shall know the truth, and the truth shall make me free (John 8:32).*

*Reflections & Prayers*

# Chapter Ten:

## *KEY LIFE AREA #8:*

### *God gives me...*
### *a Thankful Heart*

---

When we give thanks to God from the depths of our heart, we are praising and glorifying God for who He is and for all He has done in our life.

*In Christ...*

## I am thankful

*I rejoice always, pray without ceasing, and in everything give thanks; for this is the will of God in Christ Jesus for me (1 Thess. 5:16-18). I give thanks to the Lord, for He is good! For His mercy endures forever (Ps. 107:1).*

## I am content

*I enjoy my work and accept my lot in life—it is a gift from God. I don't need to look back with sorrow on my past, for God gives me joy (Eccl. 5:19b-20, TLB).*

## I am a worshipper

*I am a true worshipper and I worship the Father in spirit and in truth (John 4:23, 24). I will bless the Lord at all times; His praise shall continually be in my mouth (Ps. 34:1).*

*Reflections & Prayers*

# Conclusion

It is God's will that His children walk in wholeness and joy, living the abundant life. To live the victorious Christian life, we have established the importance of having a personal relationship with God as foundational. Built upon this solid foundation are the (8) key life areas that comprise the ingredients of true inner fulfillment.

As you continue to internalize the truths of who you are in Christ,* you will live life to the fullest with joy, perfect peace, enduring hope, purpose and meaning, and love for life, self, and others.

May the Lord bless you as you grow in your Christian walk!

In His Service,

Krystal and Violet

*The perfect companion to *God's Promises in 8 Key Life Areas that Will Change Your Life Forever!* and highly recommended to help you internalize who you are in Christ:
In Christ, I am… God's Promises on Who You Are in Christ that Will Transform You from the Inside Out

Also recommended for an in depth look at the power of renewing your mind, is: Think Like a Winner: How Renewing Your Mind with God's Word Empowers You to Win in Life

Since 1989, Krystal and Violet have been sharing and ministering God's love, hope, healing and encouragement through their books, articles, websites, businesses, music ministry and outreaches.

# About the Authors

Krystal Kuehn, MA, LPC, LLP, NCC is a psychotherapist, author, teacher, and musician.

Krystal specializes in helping people live their best life now, reach their full potential, overcome barriers, heal from their past, & develop a happiness lifestyle. Her inspirational and empowering approach has been helping people all over the world for over 20 years. Krystal's articles, poetry, and songs have been published locally and internationally. She is also the author of many books. For a complete list, go to:

http://www.amazon.com/author/krystalkuehn

Krystal has a passion for encouraging others. She believes everyone has untapped potential for greatness and everyone can live a life of fulfillment and true happiness. Krystal is the co-founder of New Day Counseling in Michigan. Her web sites include:

Christian-Kindle-Books.com
NewDayCounseling.org
NewDayCounselingCenter.blogspot.com
ChristianWalk.net
Baby-Poems.com
NewDayMusicOutreach.com
NewSongProductions.com
Facebook.com/WordsofInspiration


**Connect with Krystal Kuehn**
It is my sincerest desire and hope that *God's Promises in 8 Key Life Areas—That Will Change Your Life Forever!* has blessed you and inspired you to walk in your God-given promises and know who you are in Christ. I would love to hear your testimonials and how you have been helped. You can send your testimonials, feedback and comments to me at:

maxpotential312@gmail.com

If you would like to share your experience, I encourage you to write a review on Amazon.com

My author profile:
http://www.amazon.com/author/krystalkuehn

Join my *Words of Inspiration* page and Friend me on Facebook:
http://www.facebook.com/WordsOfInspiration

Follow and connect with me on Twitter:
http://www.twitter.com/behappy4lifeNDC

Visit my *Be Your Best* blog (offers RSS):
http://www.newdaycounselingcenter.blogspot.com/

**Violet James, MSM** is an entrepreneur, marketing and business manager, award-winning web designer, and artist. For over 20 years she has been sharing and ministering God's love, hope and healing through her books, ministries and outreaches. She is the cofounder and executive director of Christian-Kindle-Books.com, NewDayCounseling.org and NewDayMusicOutreach.com.

LinkedIn:
http://www.linkedin.com/in/violetjames

You can download *God's Promises in 8 Key Life Areas...* in AUDIO version and listen on your Kindle™ tablet, iPhone®, iPod®, and Android™. Download it at Amazon.com or Audible.com or iTunes.

## Your Free Gift

As a way of saying thanks for your purchase, we're offering this free must-have book that's exclusive to our readers.

**7 Things to Do Every Day for a Prosperous Day** *by Krystal Kuehn, MA, LPC, LLP, NCC*

Live each new day with victory and joy!!

When you subscribe to our newsletter via email, you will get free, immediate access to download the ebook.

You can download this free ebook by going here:

www.ProsperousDay.com

20611216R00035

Printed in Great Britain
by Amazon